ILLUMINATED LETTER DESIGNS
in the
HISTORIATED STYLE
of the
MIDDLE AGES

Muriel Parker

Stemmer
House
Publishers

A Barbara Holdridge book

Inquiries should be directed to
Stemmer House Publishers, Inc.
4 White Brook Road
Gilsum, NH 03448

Printed and bound in the United States of America

First Printing 1986
Second Printing 1991
Third Printing 1996
Fourth Printing 2003
Fifth Printing 2005

Colophon
Designed by Barbara Holdridge
Composed in Times Roman by Brown Composition
  Baltimore, Maryland
Printed on acid-free Williamsburg Return Card paper
  and bound by United Graphics, Inc.,
  Mattoon, Illinois

Introduction

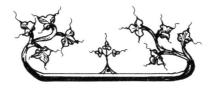

THE TERM "ILLUMINATED," in the broadest sense of the word, encompasses **illustrations** for an accompanying text, whether secular or religious. Yet there is today a difference of opinion concerning the true definition of illumination as related to manuscripts created in the Middle Ages and the ensuing Renaissance period. A good dictionary describes illumination as "decoration, as of a letter, page or manuscript, with a painted design in color, gold or silver, etc.; a design used in decoration." That would seem to cover all of the existing examples of the art. However, there are some calligraphers who firmly maintain that illumination refers only to the use of gold on vellum or parchment, since the Latin verb "illuminare," from which our word "illuminated" is derived, means to brighten or light up.

The ability of bright colors and metallic surfaces to reflect light from the page are especially pertinent to scriptural manuscripts. Divine Light of the Word of God is in essence made manifest on the pages of these treasures. There were, in fact, many books to which divine power was attributed. Elaborately embellished large gospel books, their covers encrusted with jewels and gold, were regarded as the embodiment of the presence of Christ and were often carried into the church in the opening processional, then devoutly laid on the high altar, there to be enshrined as a liturgical object of worship next to the Host.

There is little manuscript illustration that has survived from pre-Christian Roman Imperial time, when artistic expression was achieved mainly on a grander scale, such as architecture, wall paintings and mosaics. After Emperor Constantine gave official sanction to the Christian religion in 313 A.D., however, imperial patronage encouraged the building of the new basilicas in Christian communities and commissioned fifty copies of the Greek Bible. These were written and illustrated in vellum codices (book form) for the new capital of Constantinople.

A number of books have survived from these early first millenium years, and in these can be seen the strong classical influence of Roman artists. A new style of manuscript illumination eventually emerged — at first a fluid, transitional one, with gold for highlighting effects throughout. While the surviving relics of the period are regrettably fragmentary, it is possible to get an idea of the bright colors and the strength of the human figure in the pictures, called miniatures — not because of their size, which could vary from small to large, but rather due to the use of orange lead called "minium" in the painting of the illustrations. The urge to embellish letters was expressed in Byzantium during the centuries that are known as the Dark Ages. Vellum pages dyed royal purple with gold and silver letters written on them, reflected the patronage of the Imperial Court, which was characterized by pomp and ostentatious splendor. On undyed vellum as well as on the purple-dyed skins, the words written were illustrated by line drawings and colorful miniatures. As time went on it became standard to draw a miniature in the "counter" or open area of an unadorned capital letter.

The book illumination of Byzantium influenced that of the West wherever the art of illumination was still practiced, though mingled with the ornamental styles and motifs of the barbarian invaders who were gradually destroying western Roman civilization. After the sack of Rome in 410 A.D., church centers were scattered, from islands off the coast of Ireland to widely separated areas on the continent of Europe. It was in the monasteries and cloisters that learning survived these troubled centuries, known as the Dark Ages. Contemporary with the more settled Byzantine civilization, the clerical scribes of the western Christian church diligently copied the Bible and Psalter, as well as many secular books. With Latin the predominant spoken language of western Europe, Saint Jerome undertook to revise the Bible text, resulting in the Latin Vulgate Bible. This version became, over the following centuries, the essential source used by monastic scribes in the Middle Ages. However, since various sacraments were incorporated into Church litany throughout the Empire, all of the accepted liturgical forms, and additional feast days, continually created the need for new manuscripts.

Before 400 A.D., Bible texts — at least those that survived the ravages of invasions and the burning of Constantinople — were not decorated or illustrated with miniatures. A Greek Bible in the British Library, dating from the fifth century, does have pen-line decorations around the colophons of each book of the Bible, with enlarged letters at the beginning of each sentence. And after the fifth century, both Eastern and Western scribes followed the tradition of the earlier classical period, before the acceptance of the codex book form, when secular scrolls incorporated diagrams and narrative illustrations with scientific and literary texts. Following these examples, they adopted the use of miniatures within the Bible text area or as complete page illustrations.

The zeal of early Christian missionaries in converting pagan tribes inspired scribes to embellish the texts used in this work. Handsome manuscripts from the British Isles introduced continental scribal artists to fantastic examples of decorated letters with intricate designs. Examples of these are the Book of Durrow (500 A.D.), the Book of Kells (700 to 800 A.D.) and the Lindisfarne Gospels (700 A.D.), to name only a few.

During the Carolingian period (750 to 950 A.D.), scribal artists combined the miniatures of the Eastern

Byzantine manuscripts with the decorated letters of Western Insular Celtic gospel books. Since the miniatures illustrated historical Bible stories, they were called Historiated Initials. These embellished letters developed as an important part of illuminated manuscripts. Early examples exhibit definite Irish Celtic influences — interlacing, convoluted scrolls and foliage in terminals of initials, from which dragons and lion heads grow. Miniatures drawn inside open areas of the letters, though not a strong element of Celtic art, show the classical influences of artists brought from Byzantium to assist in the intellectual revival initiated by Charlemagne. During the decade between 844 and 855 A.D., historiated initials were included in many manuscripts.

The Carolingian influence flourished until the middle of the tenth century, when a steady decline of inventiveness became evident, owing to the continual disorder and internal strife brought on by the demise of the Carolingian line of kings. Schools of writing and illumination in England, Flanders, Germany and Italy kept the art of illumination alive, however.

The centuries between 1000 and 1200 A.D., bridging the Carolingian and Gothic periods, are known as the Romanesque Period. It was a time when classical influence, inspired by the mosaics of Byzantine origin, appeared in miniature drawing and painting. By this time historiated initials, known as histories or ystoires, were established elements of manuscript design. With the decrease in the monopoly of illumination by members of religious orders, professional scribes began to be employed by monasteries in the first decades of the twelfth century. The clergy was the largest market for books, but laymen of rank and wealth were also desirous of owning illustrated Psalters, commissioning them for their own libraries or to be present to churches and monasteries.

The Gothic period of the thirteenth century, overlapping the end of the Romanesque period, brought about a distinct change in illustrated books. Manuscript illuminators were directly influenced in their designs by the new style of architecture, sculpture and painted church windows. It was a time of growth in many areas. Books of every description were needed by students and professors of the new universities. Scriptoriums were not exclusively controlled by monastic societies, but were started as businesses in the citites. Craft guilds for scribes were organized.

As the fourteenth century progressed, Gothic architectural designs proliferated in books, and historiated initials within spiky Gothic canopies appeared in many manuscripts. Book illumination during this century reached a peak of splendor, with scripts, miniatures, historiated initials and borders in a decorative harmony never before achieved. Aristocratic patrons in France, Spain, Italy and England vied in acquiring exquisite manuscripts for personal libraries.

By circa 1381, Gothic illumination entered a second period of excellence and distinction, as a Courtly International style of painting developed. Severity gave way to softer, more rounded, relaxed and luxuriant forms. Birds, animals and whimsical creatures were beautifully drawn and painted. Much gold was evident. Psalters were still popular, but a new type of manuscript, the Book Of Hours (daily personal meditations), gained in popularity. The miniatures of the historiated initials depicted greater depth of space, resulting in the illusion of three-dimensionality.

With the advent of the printing press, handwritten books gradually diminished in number. Artists specializing in the design of historiated initials were no longer in great demand as they had been ever since papyrus scrolls gave way to the codex (book) form — more than a thousand years before 1455, the year of the Gutenberg Bible.

For at least fifty years following Gutenberg's invention, prestigious persons of nobility commissioned manuscripts because they believed them to be far superior to mass-produced books. The types of books desired were no longer primarily religious: books of history, chronicles, epic poems, chivalrous romances, classical historical stories, astronomy, travel, falconry and medical books were in demand. Manuscript design became luxuriant, with ornamental borders of contemporary motifs such as candelabra, swags, pearls, precious stones, cornucopia and acanthus leaves, all creating an effect of opulent richness. Workshops of every type of artist were the sources of these dazzling creations, in the brilliant period of artistic achievements known as the Renaissance.

Illuminated initials in valuable collectors' manuscripts and in royal and official charters continued to be made by hand, despite the new technology of the mass-produced book. The demand for such individually designed and executed manuscripts is in evidence to the present day.

The drawings on the pages following are planned as an abecedarium (pronounced "A B C Darium") of historiated illuminated initials: an alphabet from A to Z.

However, while examples of authentic historiated initials were used for the purpose of designing the decorated letters that enclose the "histoires" (historical pictures), the letters J, Y and Z are not found in illuminated manuscripts. These three letters, therefore, are freely drawn, incorporating several different periods of design.

The pen-and-ink renderings are not facsimiles of the original letters. They incorporate the decorative design elements of the letters and the historical pictures within the letters in ways different from the originals, but in their spirit. Readers are encouraged to create their own interpretations.

M.M.P.

Acknowledgments

My sincere gratitude is expressed to A. A. Gentile, a collector of illuminated manuscripts and books of all types, who has been singularly responsible for bringing my interest in and admiration of the beautiful art of illuminated manuscripts to the attention of Barbara Holdridge of Stemmer House Publishers, who then generously allowed me the necessary time to complete the drawings.

I wish to express my thanks to Lillian Randall, Curator of Manuscripts at the Walters Art Gallery in Baltimore, Maryland, through whose assistance the large collection of photographic copies of medieval manuscripts in the massive storehouse of the gallery library was made available to me during the months of research preceding the rendering of the drawings.

Much appreciation is deserved by my husband, Edward, for his patient supportive assistance during the hours that were spent engulfed in this book.

Bibliography

Alexander, J. J. G., *The Decorated Letter* New York: Geo. Braziller, 1978

Alexander, J. J. G., *Italian Renaissance Illuminations* New York: Geo. Braziller, 1977

Alexander, J. J. G., *The Master of Mary of Burgundy* New York: Geo. Braziller, 1970

Avril, F., *Manuscript Painting at the Court of France* New York: Geo. Braziller, 1978

Bishop, M., *The Middle Ages* New York: McGraw Hill Paperback Books, 1970

Calkins, R. G., *Illuminated Books of the Middle Ages* Ithaca, N.Y.: Cornell University Press, 1983

Calkins, R.G., *Monuments of Medieval Art* Ithaca & London: Cornell University Press, 1979

Clark, K., *Civilization* New York & Evanston: Harper & Row, 1969

Corbett, P. & Eisler, C., *The Prayer Book of Michelino da Besozzo* New York: Geo. Braziller

Csapodi-Gardonyi, K., *Europaische Buchmalerei* West Germany: Prisma Verlag, 1982

Delaisse, L. M. F., Marrow, J., & de Wit, J., *Illuminated Manuscripts, The James A. De Rothschild Collection at Waddesdon Manor* Fribourg: Office du Livre, 1977

Getty, J. Paul, Museum, *The Spinola Hours* Malibu, CA: 1984

Harthan, J., *The History of the Illustrated Book* New York: Thames & Hudson, Inc., 1981

Harthan, J., *An Introduction to Illustrated Manuscripts* Owings Mills, MD: Stemmer House, Inc., 1983

Harthan, J., *Book of Hours* New York: Thomas Crowell Co., 1977

Herbert, J. A., *Illuminated Manuscripts* New York: B. Franklin, 1969

Irblich, E. & Bise, G., *The Illuminated Naples Bible* New York: Crown Publishers, Inc., 1979

——— *Illuminated Initials Of The Gutenberg Bible* Munich: Artus Verlag, 1985

Kren, T. & Turner, D. H., *Renaissance Painting in Manuscripts* New York: Hudson Hill Press, 1983

Longnon, J., *The Tres Riches Heures of Jean, Duke of Berry* New York: Geo. Braziller, 1969

Manion, M. M. & Vines, V. F., *Illuminated Manuscripts in Australian Collections.* Melbourne, London, New York: Thames & Hudson, 1984

Marks, R. & Morgan, N., *The Golden Age of English Manuscript Painting, 1200-1500.* New York: Geo. Braziller, 1981

Meiss, M. & Beatson, E., *The Belles Heures of Jean de Berry* New York: Geo. Braziller, 1974

Meiss, M., *The Limbourgs and Their Contemporaries* New York: Geo. Braziller, 1974

Meiss, M. & Kirsch, E. W., *Visconti Hours.* New York: Geo. Braziller, 1972

Metropolitan Museum Of Art, New York, *The Cloisters Apocalypse* Zurich: Conzett & Huber, 1971

Metropolitan Museum Of Art, New York, *The Hours of Jeanne d'Evreux* Paris: Draeger Freres, 1973

——— *Ornamentation des Manuscrits au Moyen Age, 14th, 15th Centuries* Paris: R. H. Laurens, 1894

Peintner, M., *Neustifter Buchmalerei* Bozen: Verlagsanstalt Athesia, 1984

Pognon, E., *Illuminated Manuscripts of Les Tres Riches Heures du Duc de Berry* New York: Crown Publishers, Inc., 1979

Randall, L., *Illuminated Manuscripts, Masterpieces in Miniature* Schneidereith & Sons, Inc., 1984

Robb, D. M., *The Art of the Illustrated Manuscripts* Cranbury, New Jersey: A. S. Barnes, 1973

Rothe, Edith, *Mediaeval Book Illumination in Europe* London: Thames & Hudson, Ltd., 1968

Swaan, W., *The Late Middle Ages* London: Paul Elek, Ltd., 1977

Thomas, M., *The Golden Age* New York: Geo. Braziller, 1979

Thorpe, J., *The Book of Hours, Huntington Library* San Marino, CA: Anderson, Ritchie & Simon

Turner, D. H., *The Hastings Hours* London: Thames & Hudson, Ltd., 1983

Uterkircher, F., *King Rene's Book of Love* New York: Geo. Braziller, 1980

Watson, R., *The Playfair Hours, Victoria & Albert Museum* London: Westerham Press, 1984

Whalley, J. I., *Pliny the Elder, Historia Naturalis* London: Oregon Press, Ltd., 1982

Whalley, J. I., *The Student's Guide to Western Calligraphy* Colorado: Shambhaia Publications, Inc., 1984

Yapp, B. *Birds in Medieval Manuscripts* New York: Schocken Books, 1981

ue maria gracia plena

DESTO NOBIS

NGELUS

enedictus

enedicte domini

eate maria virgo

eate

omine labia mea aperies

eus qui nobis nati

Iminus illumina cio mea

omine
labia
mea
aperies
Etos
meum

eus qui de beate marie virginis

eus qui salutis

Actus est

acturus

amulorum

RATER
AMBRO
SIUS MI

RATRES·SCIENTES

elices sancti
omnes dei

aude virgo

RATIA

ODIE

ec dies quam fecit dominus

onor et

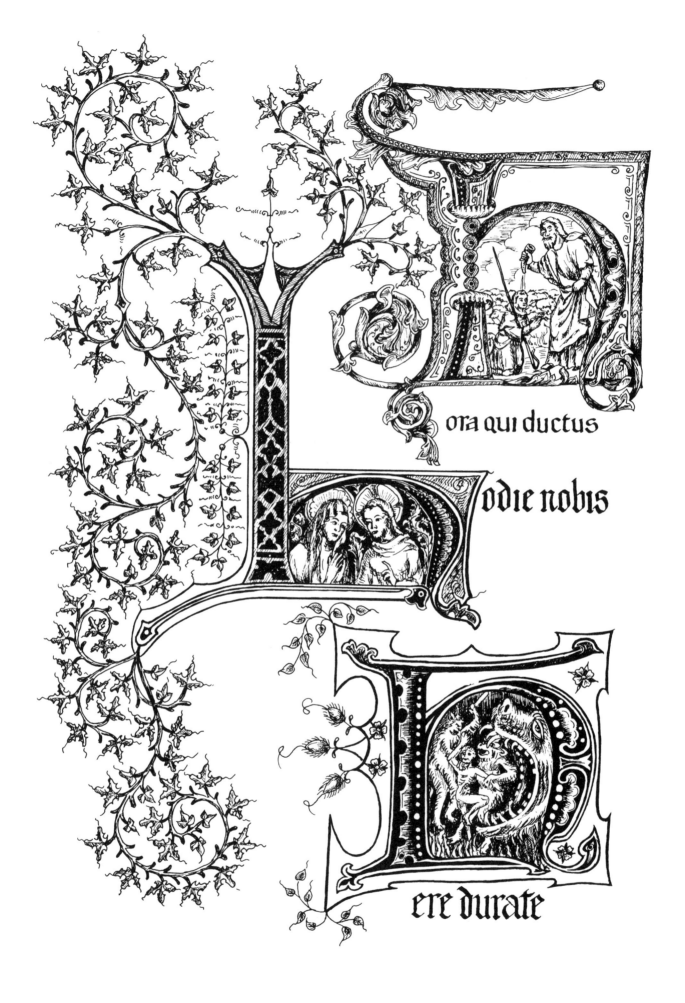

ora qui ductus

odie nobis

ere durate

N principio

n illo tempore

Nter natos

ubilate

yrie
ley
son.

yrie leyson

VRIE LEISON

yrie leison

BER

AVVATECVM

ELATVS sum ihs

egem

audent nomen

audate

iber genera

emento domine david et omnis

iſſus et gabriel

ISERERE

VLTIFARIAM

E deum laudamus:

mnipotens ſempi

mnia excelſia

MNIPOTENS

disti omnes qui operantur

Mnes leges i omnus lex

mmia excelsa tua

ver natus

ropter fratres

Atris sapienna

Ver natus est nobis

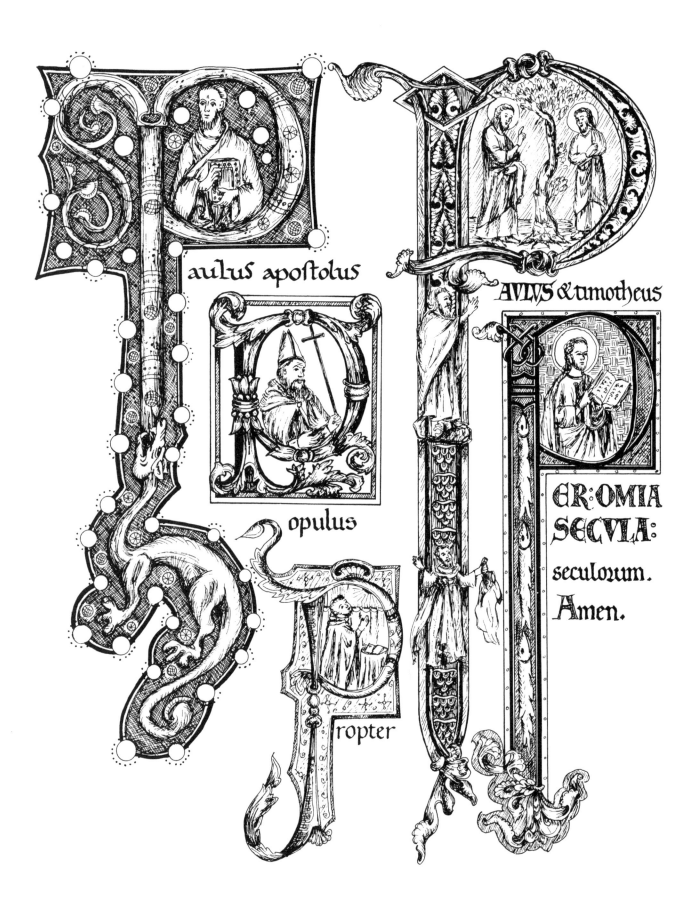

aulus apostolus

opulus

ropter

AVLVS & timotheus

ER:OMIA
SECVLA:
seculorum.
Amen.

uia ipe dixit et facta sunt ipem

VANQVAM

uoniam quide intelligere

uis est iste rex glorie

uoniam non e moreorum

Esurrea

et ad huc

tecum

egem xpistun crucifixum

equiem eternam

ogate que ad pacem

equiem eternam

Equié eter nam dona

tude at igitur intellige vuus quisq
quia situt ait salo mon. Intelligeus

ERTIVS
EXPLICIT

EVEM LAVDAMVS

E VEVM LAVDAMVS

t pacem nobis dones

t omnibus benefactoribus

ENITE adoremus

IRGO DEI GENITRIX

ENI CREATOR SPIRITUS

isdom is a fountain of life

isdom abides in the mind of a man of understanding

e are the light of the world

G ARE OF MORE VALUE

THAN MANY SPARROWS

e are the salt of the earth.......